Fosse Way

Britons and Romans in Somerset

by Peter Leach

Published by
somersethistory.co.uk
10 Society Road, Shepton Mallet BA4 5GF

The rights of Peter Leach to be identified as author of this work have been asserted by him in accordance with the Copyright Design and Patent Act 1998

Printed in Great Britain by the MPG Books Group, Bodmin and King's Lynn

ISBN 978-0-9558714-4-3

Contents

Preface

Britons and Romans along the Fosse Way takes us from the Palaeolithic to the early days of Saxon England under the guidance of Somerset's premier working archaeologist. The journey is rapidly sketched and accompanied on almost every page by photos and plans of sites, finds and landscapes. It gives up-to-date discussions of topical issues as well as a solid factual review. The focus is on the top end of Somerset, especially on the Fosse Way - that curious Roman road that goes for no particular reason in a more or less straight line from Exeter to Lincoln. Bath and Ilchester lie at either end of the road in our area, but most attention is paid to the settlement at Shepton Mallet, essentially newly discovered by the author fewer than 20 years ago.

Our guide, Peter Leach, has been digging in Somerset since the 1970s, directing huge excavations at Ilchester and Shepton Mallet, and more modestly scaled explorations at Taunton and South Cadbury Castle amongst a host of other Somerset sites. Further afield he has dug in the Midlands and, abroad, on the Adriatic Dalmatian coast. My own Somerset archaeology began at his second Ilchester dig. This was out in the town's suburbs and involved a vast area which Peter had divided into almost 100 Roman-numeralled areas. (As you will see from the account of the Shepton Mallet excavations, Peter is very fond of Roman numerals.) What I recall most of that excavation was the litany of cries: 'Anyone know where Area LXXVI is?'

Peter is no lofty bookish director but by far the best hands-on excavator I have ever seen at work. He must also be the Somerset archaeologist who has visited more sites in the field than many others. His knowledge of Britain's field monuments is absolutely encyclopaedic. Some might think that to spend your time on your knees in all weathers excavating pits and postholes would be enough archaeology, but Peter will, during an excavation or not, have always just added visiting some more sites to his list.

Times have changed in archaeology. Once the very activity was challenged by developers who saw it as an annoyance. TV exposure has changed all that, but Peter has also played a patient part in educating planners and developers. We once calmed a local authority planner by saying that we had both worked in the City and so were well aware of the pressurised world of high finance. What we omitted to say was that our experience was of working on the City of London waterfront digs in the early 70s for the subsistence wage thought appropriate at the time by the Ministry of Public Buildings and Works!

The archaeology of Fosse Lane was so utterly unexpected that it threw all the current systems of planning and archaeology into disarray. I recall standing with Peter in 1990 in the middle of that huge area stripped of topsoil which was everywhere a treasure house of Roman archaeology - coins, pottery, walls, buildings and so on, and for which there was pitifully inadequate provision and a deadline to hand over the site that was six weeks away. Anyone looking at the Fosse Lane 1990 report that Peter produced must really marvel that so much was achieved. To some extent the circumstances of that dig - the imminent destruction and the anger of the protesters - must have some bearing on the bizarre story of the faked amulet. This must have been one of those moments when someone lost all contact with reality - a kind of moral panic. It seems that we may never know the true story.

The following pages represent a timely overview of the archaeology of the Shepton Mallet area, linking us back to the Romans and from the Romans back to the crucial early millennia, the lessons of which we disregard at our peril. Our settlements, our daily lives, the objects we use, and our attitude to our surroundings make so much more sense when set in the long timescale of this story. Although we believe that everything we do is new, in fact we really only do little more than what people have always done.

Peter Ellis MA, FSA Honorary editor Somerset Archaeology and Natural History

Introduction

Archaeology and archaeological discoveries have a relatively high profile in modern popular culture. A fascination with the past and its remains has a long history in Britain, with origins in the Renaissance and the antiquarians of the 17th and 18th centuries, to an expanding Victorian engagement combined with increasing scientific respectability. In our own day archaeology's public profile and popularity is at an all-time high, thanks largely to intelligent and informative television presentation through such programmes as *Time Team* and *Meet the Ancestors*, or well-made and wide-ranging documentaries; relatively frequent press coverage, and an expanding range of literature from the popular to more technical and academic treatises. This high profile has been matched in the public sector by increasing recognition and protection/conservation of archaeological resources.

The statutory protection of remains selected for their outstanding importance, Ancient Monuments, goes back to the late 19th century, but in the past few decades the scope of protection and conservation has expanded above all through local authorities. In Somerset the Historic Environment Service of the County Council provides advice to District Council planning authorities and developers, among others, on the potential archaeological implications of development, and maintains an extensive database of information - the Heritage Environment Record - for public access and consultation (see www.somerset.gov.uk/heritage).

The richness and diversity of Somerset's archaeology has been particularly well served and amply demonstrated over the past few decades by new discoveries, both through excavations and in more wide-ranging surveys. The latter have included extensive coverage of areas such as Exmoor, the Quantocks, Somerset's historic towns, parts of the Somerset Levels, and currently Mendip, while more intensive survey techniques have been pioneered at Shapwick or in the environs of South Cadbury Castle. There has never been excavation and discovery on such a scale as in Somerset today, much of it a direct result of responses to new development and the consequent obligation of developers, through archaeological contractors, to investigate and record archaeological remains on their sites. No less important, however, are the research motivated investigations, as in the Somerset wetlands or the southern Quantocks, occasional contributions by *Time Team*, the increasing

Part of the Shapwick hoard found in1998, the largest hoard of Roman silver coin found in Britain.

contribution of local community-based projects, metal detectorists, and not least unexpected chance discoveries.

Among the more spectacular discoveries have been prehistoric wooden trackways across the Somerset Levels, a Bronze Age village at Brean Down, a Bronze Age shield at South Cadbury and exploration of Cadbury Castle, prehistoric gold ornaments from near Priddy on Mendip, or the enormous hoard of Roman silver coins from Shapwick. In the post-Roman period, excavations of the Saxon and medieval royal palaces at Cheddar, exploration of the origins and development of Wells cathedral, or more recently excavation of the medieval priory and its burials in Taunton stand out. Somerset is renowned for its wealth of late Roman villas, and several new discoveries at Lopen, Dinnington and Yarford, near Kingston St Mary, have hit the headlines in recent years.

Not least among these has been the discovery at Fosse Lane, on the edge of Shepton Mallet, of a small and all but unknown Roman town. This site and some of the others, have been the subject of academic style reports, but the volume of archaeological discovery across the county has also stimulated the production of more wide-ranging and accessible publications. These have included a recent updated survey of the county *The Archaeology of Somerset*, eds. Chris Webster and Tom Mayberry, Somerset County Council 2007; *Roman Somerset* by Peter Leach, The Dovecote Press 2001; *Mendip's Past* by Penny Stokes, Mendip District Council 1999; or *The Field Archaeology of Exmoor* by Hazel Riley and Robert Wilson-North, 2001, and *The Historic Landscape of the Quantock Hills* by Hazel Riley, 2006, both published by English Heritage. A current Mendip survey by English Heritage may be the subject of a similar publication, while publication of The *Archaeology of Mendip*, ed. Jodie Lewis, University of Worcester (Heritage Publications), highlighting recent research is imminent. A more extensive list of relevant publications is given at the end of this book.

A dolphin depicted on a mosaic floor at the Lopen Roman villa, found in 2001

My archaeological involvement with the Fosse Way began over 30 years ago around Ilchester, in an era of major road-building schemes then affecting Somerset (M5, A303 improvements, etc.), and the birth of modern rescue archaeology that was to evolve into strategies for conservation and management of our archaeological/heritage resources in place today.

In 1990 I was reacquainted with the road a dozen miles or so further north near Shepton Mallet, where the pressures of commercial development provided an opportunity to reveal and explore what was to all intents and purposes a previously unknown Roman settlement beside it. Continuing developments have provided further opportunities to continue these investigations, and most recently renewed controversy surrounding one of the outstanding discoveries of the 1990 excavations, 'the Amulet', has come to the fore. Equally important have been the glimpses of earlier prehistoric ancestors and their activities around Fosse Lane and Shepton Mallet, or research through a local community-based project centred upon Beacon Hill, where the Fosse Way crosses the Mendip ridge to the north. Some of these discoveries have been the subject of detailed publications and more will follow, while in the wider context of the environs of Mendip and the Fosse Way, there has been a notable focus for a wide range of archaeological investigations and discoveries over the past two decades.

By no means all of these researches and discoveries will be readily or widely available, but at the risk of repetition I hope in this book to make many of them more accessible to a wider public, to better illuminate their context and significance, and to pull together some of the threads which link these remains of a seemingly remote and distant past to our lives and society today. Unlike history, archaeology rarely gives us names or narrative, but can nevertheless provide a glimpse into lives and behaviour not so very far removed from our own. A little more than 60 generations take us back into pre-Roman Britain, to people who for some will have been ancestors, and whose lives and occupations still influence our 21st-century environment.

Map of the Fosse Way and its environs on the Mendip Hills

Beginnings

Climate change and predictive scenarios of its effects are becoming hot topics for us all, but around 13,000 years ago Britain and the northern hemisphere of our planet was subjected to a change of almost unimaginable magnitude. Contrary to formerly held theories, recent scientific studies suggest the end of the last Ice Age to have been very sudden, coming about within perhaps just a few short years rather than over centuries or millennia. While the reasons and mechanisms behind this are less well understood, one effect of a rapid rise in temperatures was to encourage human communities to migrate northwards back into Britain, at that time still a large peninsula at the northwest corner of Europe. Modern genetics is revolutionising our picture of how and when Britain was re-colonised, but perhaps remarkably, until the advent of more widespread modern immigrations, around 70% of the indigenous British population seem to have originated with two main movements of Stone Age hunter-gatherers from Europe, up the western seaboards, or across what was later to become the North Sea.

Lower Palaeolithic chert handaxe found near Taunton

Prior to this, the severity of the glacial environment, even beyond the permanent ice sheets, would rule out any established human settlement in Britain for thousands of years. But there were visitors and settlers here in warmer periods before that time, evidence for some of the earliest in Britain coming from the Mendip Hills. At **Westbury Quarry** near Wells ancient cave deposits preserved flint and chert tools and cut bones in association with other animal remains, including Sabre-toothed tiger and Rhinoceros, indicative of early hominids in the area from around 0.5 million years ago when the climate was warmer. Elsewhere in Somerset distinctive flint and chert handaxes of **Lower Palaeolithic** type, found mainly near Taunton, Watchet and Chard, suggest further groups of hunter-gatherers around 400,000-300,000 years ago. Evidence thereafter is sparse, but there are tools indicating the occasional presence of Neanderthal hunters in Somerset. Some of the best evidence comes from the Hyena Den at **Wookey Hole** associated with animal remains suggesting a temporary hunting camp here some 40,000 years ago.

Uphill, near Weston-super-Mare

The earliest evidence for modern humans comes from **Uphill Cave** at the western end of Mendip, where a bone spear has been dated to between 29,000 and 27,000 years old. Evidence and remains of these **Upper Palaeolithic** hunters have been found elsewhere in Britain, and finds of flint tools show that they also used the **Cheddar Gorge** caves while hunting across the Mendip Hills, but they were almost certainly driven from our shores with the onset of the last great ice age from about 25,000 years ago. Some of the latest re-colonisers of Britain at the end of the last ice age certainly came to Cheddar, where remains of perhaps the earliest established human settlement in Somerset have been found in **Gough's Cave**. Sadly, many of the earlier discoveries here were lost or poorly recorded, but more recent work suggests that a small community of hunters may have spent the harsher winter months here over several centuries around 11,000 BC. Even with rapidly rising temperatures at the end of the last ice age, the climate could be unpredictable, and there was a partial return to colder conditions for several centuries until around 10,000 years ago. From then until the present day the climate has been relatively stable and temperate, encouraging the establishment and spread of human communities.

View down Cheddar Gorge

A temperate climate brought big changes to both the fauna and flora of Britain, with the spread of extensive deciduous forests and a consequent change in the animals inhabiting it. Gone were the Reindeer and Woolly Mammoth, to be replaced by Red Deer, Wild Boar and Aurochs (wild cattle) among others. Perhaps most devastating of all was the enormous rise in sea levels resulting from the massive glacial ice melt, far outstripping any rises predicted for the near future today. Vast tracts of land beneath the North Sea and along the English Channel, in particular, were inundated, the new **Mesolithic** colonisers and communities were forced onto higher ground, and the British Isles, separated from mainland Europe, came into being again. Locally, the Bristol Channel was formed, and eventually the rising water levels overwhelmed the lowland oak forests to the west of Mendip converting them to the wetlands of the Somerset Levels.

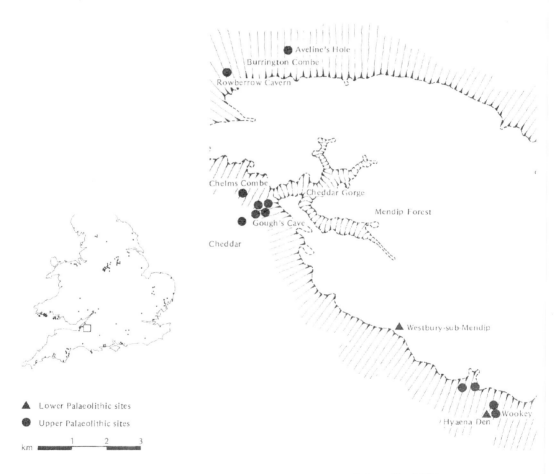

Some Palaeolithic cave sites on the Mendip Hills

Britons

The new Mesolithic hunters and harvesters of the temperate forests soon spread widely throughout the newly formed British Isles, although their remains are often elusive. Living as mobile hunters and gatherers of food, permanent settlements did not exist, although traces of temporary seasonal encampments have been found. More common are their distinctive flint artefacts, examples of which have been found widely across the Mendip Hills. A notable concentration from **Chedzoy** 'island' near Bridgwater could indicate one such encampment, doubtless exploiting the rich resources of the Levels. Scattered finds across the uplands of Exmoor, the Mendip, and the

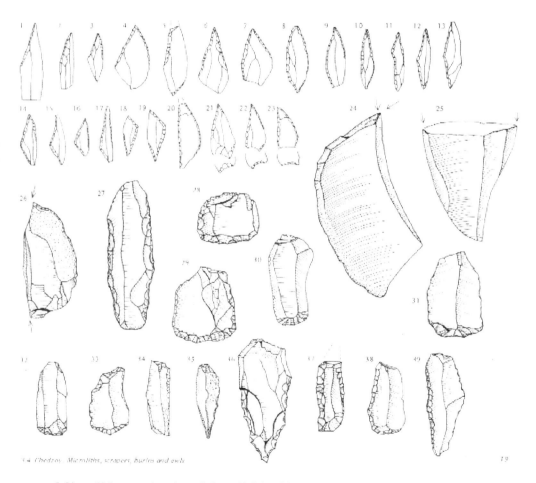

Microliths and other Mesolithic flint tools found near Chedzoy

Quantock Hills suggest that these were hunting territories and that there was some partial clearance of the forests there. Some of the Mendip cave sites were also reused, apparently now for burial, as at **Avelines Hole** in Burrington Combe. This is still the largest Mesolithic burial site known in Britain, containing over 70 bodies, though sadly many were destroyed in Bristol during Word War II. Recently this cave hit the headlines with the discovery of what may be contemporary carved designs on one wall, and another carving of perhaps the same date has been recognised at **Long Hole** in Cheddar Gorge. These are later than the more famous representational cave art in France and Spain, but equivalent animal carvings have been found in the Derbyshire **Cresswell Crags** caves, so could Cheddar's caves yet contain further surprises? At least one burial was made in Goughs Cave, Cheddar, around 9000 years ago, where the remains of a young man discovered in 1903 is displayed in the museum there. The recent recovery of DNA from these bones demonstrated a direct link with a present day inhabitant of Cheddar, dramatic illustration of our ancestral connections!

Avelines Hole entrance, Burrington Combe

Britain and Europe were finally parted by the sea around 7000 years ago, but some immigration continued and links were maintained. Eventually these contacts brought some revolutionary new ideas, the domestication of animals and the cultivation of plants, the **Neolithic** revolution. Quite how sudden the introduction of this new economic system really was is still unclear. Certainly at first its impact on Britain was relatively limited, and its appearance from around 4000 BC here probably came about through the long-established and maintained links with the continent rather than any great influx of invaders or immigrants.

Reconstruction of the Sweet Track at Westhay, the oldest dated trackway in Britain

Pastoralists

One of the earliest and most precise dates for Neolithic activity in England comes from Somerset - the date of 3807/6BC from timber used to build a wooden trackway - the **Sweet Track** - through the marshes to link the Polden Hills with an 'island' at Westhay in the Somerset Levels. These wetlands were already an important resource for local Mesolithic communities, and their continuing value as sources of food (e.g. fish, wildfowl, wild plants) or of raw materials (timber, rushes, etc.), are evidenced by later prehistoric trackways and even habitations, as at the Iron Age Glastonbury and Mere lake villages. However, it was the uplands where most people lived during Neolithic times, although the evidence is often hard to come by. Growing crops and keeping animals for food gave the Neolithic way of life a significant advantage over its predecessors and was the spur for a substantial increase in population and new colonisation of the land over the next millennium and more. This economic revolution was marked by new implements; notably stone, flint tools and pottery; new burial sites and practices; new places of assembly and ritual; and the progressive clearance or conversion of Britain's natural forest environment to pasture, on the better drained uplands at least.

Despite changes in lifestyle and a steadily growing population, finding the sites and remains of Neolithic settlements in Britain has always been difficult. One reason may be that people were more mobile; animal husbandry was probably the economic basis for most communities, while arable cultivation was relatively less important, depending upon regular changes of locality to guarantee soil fertility as fresh land was cleared, rather than the maintenance of permanent fields. Another may be the character of buildings, usually of timber and perhaps seasonal or built to last no more than a few seasons at any one site. Large rectangular timber-framed halls are found in parts of Europe, and occasionally in Britain, while stone was used in some areas, perhaps most famously on the Orkney Islands, where are preserved some of the oldest known houses at sites like **Skara Brae**.

In our region the discoveries of living sites are few and far between, and most often arise by accident during the course of investigating remains of later periods. One of the most convincing was a circular building defined by post-holes found on the site of the Roman Villa excavated at **Chew Park** before its inundation beneath the Chew Valley Lake in the 1950s. More difficult to

Neolithic pottery and a polished stone axe from Cornwall in a pit at South Cadbury

interpret are pits or other features, which are identified when associated with pottery, stone and flint tools, animal or plant food remains. Examples include a site disturbed by the remains of Wells' earlier Anglo-Saxon cathedral, pits found in advance of stone quarrying at **Doulting** with pottery, animal bone deposits and a radiocarbon date centring around 2500 BC, or on the new **Tadley Acres** housing development south of Shepton Mallet where one containing burnt hazelnut shells was radiocarbon dated to around 2900 BC. Many pits of this type contain deposits that appear to be very deliberately placed or associated together, suggesting a symbolic function, perhaps as settlement site or territorial markers rather than for refuse disposal, even though there may rarely be any clear evidence of buildings or other activity nearby. Sometimes it is only the survival of their distinctive and very durable flint or stone implements (stone and flint axes, flint arrowheads or knives and scrapers) which are found scattered across ploughed fields or on later sites, which suggest a primary Neolithic presence in the landscape. Excavations along **Fosse Lane** near Shepton Mallet for example, recovered an extensive

Neolithic flint implements from the Fosse Lane settlement site,
Shepton Mallet

collection of Neolithic material from among the Roman remains, though no recognised structures.

Our Neolithic ancestors and pioneers did leave more visible and sometimes dramatic markers of their presence in and ownership of the landscape. Some of the earliest were connected with death and burial, as represented by monuments known as long barrows. These long mounds of earth or stone rubble were largely built within the earlier centuries of the 4th millennium BC, to contain the remains of a selection of their local communities.

Relatively few of these monuments survive across Somerset, except here in the northeast corner of the county. Best known is at **Stoney Littleton**, near Wellow, where the restored mound (cared for by English Heritage) contains a low, stone slab-lined and capped passage, with side chambers or transepts that originally contained human remains. Others in ruinous condition are known around Frome, **Fromefield, Rhode, Orchardleigh, Buckland Down,** or further west at **Chew Down** and the **Fairy Toot** at Nempnett Thrubwell, many now all but destroyed. These tombs are at the southern edge of the distribution of a type known as Cotswold-Severn long barrows, found across the Cotswolds and South Wales but barely reaching the Mendip Hills. Those few

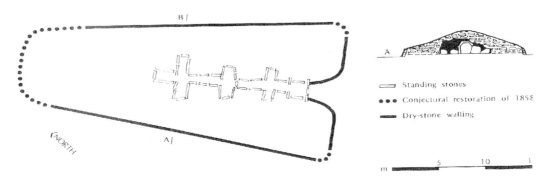

Plan of the Neolithic chambered burial mound at
Stoney Littleton, near Wellow

long barrows identified on Mendip may not have contained stone chambers, there are two near **Priddy** and at least one on **Pen Hill** above Wells; another badly damaged example closer to the Fosse Way at Charmborough, Holcombe, is known as **Giant's Grave**. None have been investigated by modern archaeological methods and there may yet be other undiscovered examples on Mendip, whose lighter soils would surely have been attractive to Neolithic communities.

Long barrows were more than just burial places, probably acting as centres for communal ritual and perhaps symbolising the identity of individual groups as markers on their land and their claim upon it via the ancestors.

Later in Neolithic society expressions of symbolism and ritual suggest an evolution towards the inclusion of more extended communities or tribes through the construction of great circular stone, earth or timber monuments, known collectively as henges. Several of these can be found on Mendip, surviving as upstanding circular earthen banks with an inner ditch often still visible; the most impressive being the four **Priddy circles** near the Castle of Comfort Inn, ranging between 150m and 170m in diameter. None are yet known further east, although smaller levelled examples occasionally come to light, as at **East Lambrook** in south Somerset. The most famous of these sites are of course **Stonehenge** and **Avebury** in Wiltshire, where the stone settings further enhance their impact and significance. In our region a site of perhaps comparable importance is **Stanton Drew** in the valley of the River Chew south of Bristol. Here survive one large and two smaller stone circles, several outlying stone settings, and dramatic evidence below ground for multiple timber settings around the largest circle. The latter were found by geophysical survey, which also detected an encircling ditch comparable to that marking the first phase at Stonehenge, around 3000BC.

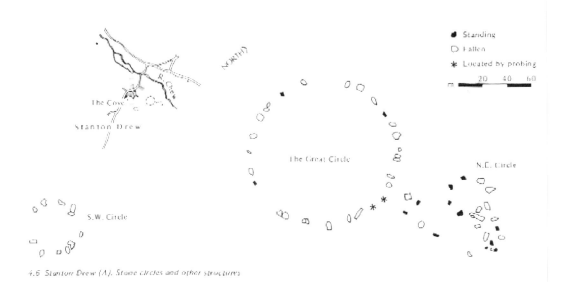

4.5 Stanton Drew (A). Stone circles and other structures

Stanton Drew, plan of the stone circles

Stone circle at Stanton Drew

Metal Workers

The appearance of monuments like this imply not only a growing population but also the evolution of a more complex society, where large numbers of people could be motivated for the effort required to build them. At the end of the Neolithic this growth in population, at a time when the climate was slightly warmer and dryer than today, combined with a new element, the appearance of metal, was to have an even greater impact upon human economy and society in Britain. The **Bronze Age** is usually recognised as beginning from around 2200 BC, although copper and its alloy, bronze, and more rarely gold, made occasional appearances two or three centuries earlier. Styles of pottery changed also, and one particularly distinctive type **Beaker pottery** seems to be closely associated with the appearance of metal and probably, a limited immigration of new people from different parts of Europe. The presence of this style of pottery at ceremonial sites like the Priddy circles or another henge at **Gorsey Bigbury** above Cheddar Gorge, suggests some continuity with the communities and traditions of the past, but big changes were afoot.

Perhaps the most visible and enduring symbol of our Bronze Age ancestors

Bronze Age round barrows on Beacon Hill

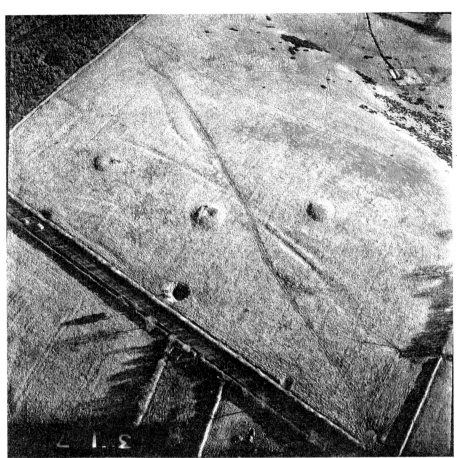

Beacon Hill round barrows from the air, the mound visible in the trees (top left) was excavated in 2007-08

were their burial places, notably the round barrow mounds that still survive scattered across Mendip and neighbouring hills. The great majority were built between roughly 2100 BC and 1500 BC, most often for the burial of single individuals. Some of these survive in groups or cemeteries of barrows on high ground, as on **North Hill** above Priddy or **Beacon Hill** above Shepton Mallet. Although of later construction, the location of the Priddy Nine Barrows and Ashen Hill cemeteries, and a general concentration of barrows in that locality, was probably influenced by the presence of the late Neolithic ceremonial henge circles. No such focus is known further east, but around Beacon Hill there are smaller but significant scatters and groups. These include another linear cemetery on **Small Down Knoll**, Evercreech, a group near **Cranmore**, a few individual examples around Shepton Mallet, and others to the north near Chilcompton and Ston Easton. The larger barrow groups like Beacon Hill evidently developed over several centuries, as foci for

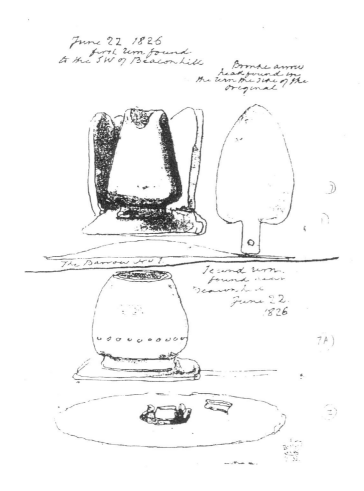

Rev. John Skinner's sketch of Early Bronze Age cremation urns and a bronze razor from barrows excavated by him on Beacon Hill in 1826

multiple burials, into the later Bronze Age, and perhaps as special areas for the dead and the ceremonies connected with their burial and remembrance. Their hilltop sites suggest special places away from the living though still highly visible. Elsewhere, smaller groups or individual barrows, often less prominently sited, may be more closely associated with specific settlements.

Round barrows have long been recognised as burial places, and have attracted the attention of treasure seekers as well as antiquarians for many centuries. This has resulted in a relatively large amount of information gained and material recovered, although sadly much of this was poorly recorded and many of the finds are lost. The prominent Beacon Hill barrows attracted early attention, although their first excavators left few records. The Rev. John Skinner, vicar of Camerton was the most active, excavating several barrows and recording their condition and his discoveries, along with illustrations, in his diaries during the 1820s.

'They had not commenced digging ten minutes to the south of the Beacon, where I had found an urn three years ago, in the space of half an hour they came to a large urn the mouth resting on a flat stone. The bottom had been injured by the pressure of the earth above it, although guarded by a flat stone, as were the sides by a cist of upright stones. Wishing the Bishop should see the urn and its contents when opened I dispatched a messenger to Wells leaving the vessel to harden in the sun and air and employed the men in the interval at another place. Which seemed to have been the site of a barrow, although all the earth and stones which formed the tumulus had been removed. I was not disappointed, for in the course of a few minutes the men came up to a large stone about two feet in length and fourteen inches in thickness, placed just below the surface of the soil. Under this was a thin flat stone of the Pennant kind and just below this the urn, which was of a different shape to that first discovered, being wider at the mouth and not so high, it was also reversed on a flat stone. This I had dug round and left for the Bishops inspection, who was delighted with our mornings good fortune. We proceeded to the examination of one of the large barrows adjoining or rather contiguous to that opened three years since, it had some large stones in the centre, but no urn or ashes. We found a bronze arrow head, almost two inches long and one wide, in the first urn among the bones which half filled the vessel. In the second urn there was nothing but ashes and the clay was so much decayed we found it impossible to send it to Wells. Some men with a hand barrow dispatched by the Bishop on his return, conveyed the first in safety to the place of its destination during the night with some large fragments of the second.'
June 22, 1826

This part of Skinner's account relates to the opening of three barrows now towards the eastern end of Beacon Wood. Even at this time he noted that some of the barrows appeared to have been dug into, perhaps in earlier searches for treasure. Several years later in 1840 the Gentleman's Magazine (January 1841) recorded that: *'Mr Rugg of Lapwing farm, between Oakhill and Shepton Mallet, in digging over a tumulus lately came to some stones, in removing which he discovered a few sepulchral urns of very rude workmanship containing bones and ashes. In digging further he discovered more, in all 12-14. The farm is situated on what is called the Beacon near some very*

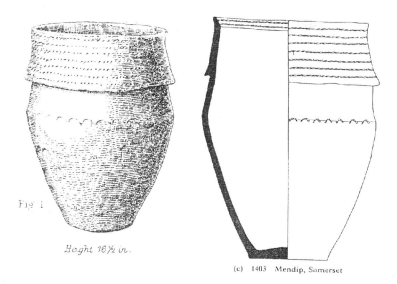

Fig 1

Height 16½ in.

(c) 1403 Mendip, Somerset

Early Bronze Age Collared Urn from Beacon Hill, now in Birmingham Museum

extensive ancient Roman entrenchment's called Masbury camp and there are several other tumuli near.' - This account apparently relates to the most westerly of the barrows now within the open field west of the wood.

From these accounts and the commentary of later visitors and recorders of the barrows it is evident that much has been lost or destroyed, a process which continued well into the 20th century through forestry clearance and replanting. An attempt to salvage some remains in advance of this destruction resulted in further excavation of two of the barrows dug earlier by Skinner, by local schoolmaster Max Unwin (Curator of the Shepton Mallet Museum) in 1953. This apparently recovered two more cinerary urns of Early Bronze Age type and some pottery of later Bronze Age date, the whereabouts of which is regrettably now unknown. One of the few vessels to survive from Beacon Hill is a Collared Urn of Early Bronze Age type in the City Museum, Birmingham, which may be one of those found by farmer Rugg. This, and other vessels illustrated by Skinner are a good indication that many of the barrows were probably raised at that time, perhaps soon after 2000 BC. This is supported by the *bronze arrow head* from one urn, actually a bronze razor of the period. Thanks to Skinners' notes we also know that most bodies were cremated, and that stone slabs or small cists enclosed or capped the vessels. Records of a dozen or more urns from farmer Rugg's excavation

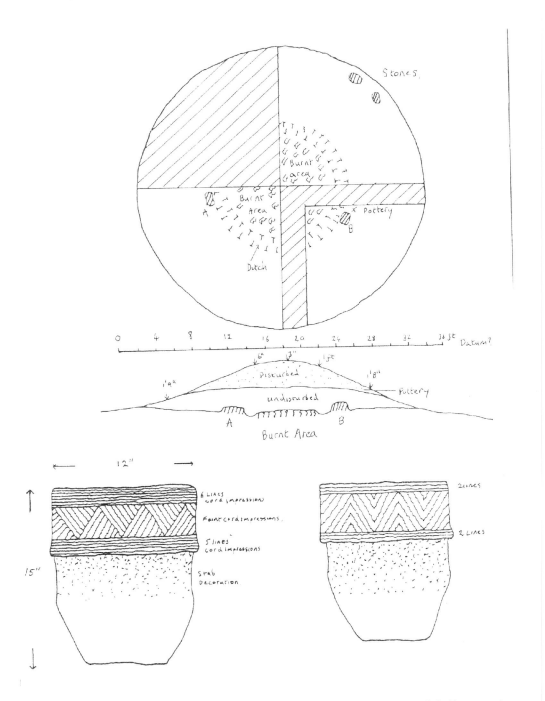

Sketch of a barrow excavated at Barren Down, Shepton Mallet, and two EBA cremation urns

suggest that the barrows were used for multiple burials, probably over a long period, while some of the pottery found by Max Unwin was apparently of Middle Bronze Age type.

In 2007 there was an opportunity to put some of these early discoveries into a properly recorded and scientifically supported context as part of a local community archaeology project organised through the Beacon Hill Society, which helps to care for and research the history of the wood here (see www.bhsm.org.uk). An excavation trench across a damaged barrow close to the western edge of the wood discovered an undisturbed cremation urn of Middle Bronze Age (Deverel Rimbury) type, containing the remains of a young woman dated by radio carbon to around 1600 BC, and charcoal from her funeral pyre. There was nothing else buried with her but the pot was set into the base of a large pit, capped by a slab of sandstone and covered by further blocks of stone. The pit was cut into the top of the barrow as a later feature, and may lie above an intact Early Bronze Age primary burial contemporary with the barrow.

The mound itself was constructed of turfs cut from the surrounding hill, and the analysis of pollen recovered from these and a soil buried beneath suggests that although trees like Oak, Elm, Ash, Birch and Alder were growing locally, with a Hazel understory, plants like heather, grasses and occasional weeds of cultivation indicate that the hilltop was open heathland, which seems to have been burnt off before the turves were cut. As it happens, the excavation of another round barrow a few kilometres to the north at **Old Down** near Chilcompton, was undertaken around the same time by a team from the University of Worcester. Here was found another cremation accompanied by a miniature vessel of Early Bronze Age type, probably representing the primary interment.

Other remains of local inhabitants from this time have been found at Shepton Mallet. Two round barrows, still visible as low mounds at **Barren Down** just north of the town, were also excavated by Max Unwin in 1953. Primary cremations were found centrally beneath both, one of a child and the other in a shallow rock-cut cist grave, and both were associated with pyre material. No pottery vessels were recorded and regrettably the whereabouts of these finds now are again unknown. In 1934 a new tennis court was being laid out in the

Excavation of a barrow in Beacon Wood 2007:

Turf preserved in the barrow mound (top);

sandstone slab (middle)

sealing an intact Middle Bronze Age cremation urn (bottom)

The restored Middle Bronze Age, Deverell Rimbury cremation urn from Beacon Wood 2007

garden of 'Greenacres', one of the (then) new houses being built along Compton Road, on the south side of the town. The earthmoving revealed a small rock-cut pit containing the crouched skeleton of a man, some flint flakes and fragments of Early Bronze Age pottery. Some of these remains were deposited in the County Museum at Taunton; was this perhaps the site of another long vanished round barrow?

Farmers

The remains of the dead and their burial places may be relatively well known, but what of the living in the Bronze Age? As in the Neolithic, evidence for domestic settlements, houses or lifestyles continues to be very sparse, reflecting perhaps relatively impermanent structures and a continuing degree of mobility for many communities. A rare example buried by sand was excavated a few years ago at **Brean Down**, where a small settlement of circular houses was preserved. But with a still growing population and evidence for some climatic deterioration towards the middle of the second millennium BC, prehistoric societies in Britain underwent radical change; as revolutionary perhaps as the introduction of agriculture had been over 2000 years previously. In essence these pressures are reflected in increased land clearance, the widespread appearance of fields and boundaries, and more permanent and visible settlements. But also in the more extensive manufacture and use of bronze in weapons and implements, quantities of which were deposited in bogs or rivers, notably in and around the **Somerset Moors**. Recent discover-

Excavating a Bronze Age roundhouse at Brean Down in 1985

Clay mould for a Late Bronze Age socketed axe from a bronze casting site at Sigwells near South Cadbury

ies near **South Cadbury** have located Late Bronze Age weapon moulds and a casting site, one product of which was a sword found in the 19th century during construction of the Midsomer Norton railway station.

Effectively, all this began a process that has evolved into the settled rural landscapes of fields, woodland or waste, permanent villages and farms that we know today. Necessarily, the evidence for these origins has been almost obliterated by continuing landscape development since then, although ancient clues are sometimes preserved in patterns of tracks, land divisions or settlement sites down to the present day. One of the effects of the Bronze Age expansion was the clearance and settlement of more marginal land, some of which reverted to lowland heaths like those in Dorset and the New Forest, or the moorlands of Exmoor and Dartmoor, when the land became impover-ished and the climate deteriorated. One benefit of this process has been the preservation of evidence for these first settlers in the form of their houses, fields, burial sites, ceremonial monuments, and, sometimes, environmental material.

The evidence preserved in the higher parts of Dartmoor is exceptional in this respect, giving a vivid picture of the character and lifestyles of its Bronze Age

Middle and Late Bronze enclosures excavated at Gore End Farm, Shepton Mallet, 2004

inhabitants and an idea of what has been lost elsewhere. Similar processes and remains might be expected in other upland areas like the Mendip Hills or on Salisbury Plain, but much of the evidence here will have been lost through later agriculture.

If we are lucky, archaeology may still give us glimpses of the origins and early stages of these processes on lower, more fertile lands, as on the site of the **Field Farm** housing development south of Shepton Mallet. Occasional pits containing a little Neolithic or Early Bronze Age pottery probably signify some occupation and settlement in this locality before 3000 BC, however elusive the sites and remains of houses or other structures may be. Later in the Bronze Age the focus begins to sharpen and by the middle of the second millennium BC we have evidence of field plots, domestic animals, crops and hints of the rituals and religious beliefs associated with these things.

Between Field Farm and Collett Park excavation in advance of the housing development uncovered part of an enclosure defined by deep, curving rock-cut ditches, with an entrance causeway, that contained several pits and structures defined by post holes. Pottery and radiocarbon dates suggest intermittent use between around 1400 BC and 1000 BC, perhaps as a settlement or place for herding animals. At Gore End Farm, just north of the Cannards Grave roundabout, were the remains of another partial enclosure defined by segments of curving rock-cut ditches, whose phases of use spanned a similar period. In its earlier Middle Bronze Age phase the site is associated with the fragmentary surviving remains of fields and boundaries, as well as animal remains including two complete cow burials, part of a sheep, and later a human burial, that were placed in the terminals of several of the ditches. In its Late Bronze Age phase (around 1000-900 BC) the earlier site was levelled and there was a new arrangement of ditches and pits, with a causeway between the two largest ditches emphasised by two flanking entrance posts. Within the incomplete enclosure was a D-shaped structure or building defined by postholes, one containing a clay loomweight. The ditches contained animal bone, pottery and charcoal that were especially concentrated at the causeway terminals. Much of this had been dumped as part of a final levelling of the site, while the material itself suggests the residue of feasting events that may have been associated with the post-built structure inside the enclosure. The environmental evidence suggests an essentially open landscape, where sheep, cattle, pig and horse were kept, and there was local cultivation of spelt and bread wheat, and possibly oats and barley.

Middle Bronze Age cow burial in a ditch terminal, Gore End Farm, Shepton Mallet, 2004

Late Bronze Age pottery from Gore End Farm, Shepton Mallet, 2004

Both sites lay close to a small stream that flows north to join the River Sheppey, apparently within a system of contemporary fields. The evidence for ritual and ceremony at Gore End Farm suggests that this was its prime function throughout, rather than as a domestic settlement, an interpretation

Prehistoric field system banks near East Compton

reinforced by the more recent discovery of the remains of a round barrow and cremation burials with pottery urns of Middle Bronze Age type barely a stones throw away to the south. Perhaps this was a place of occasional assembly or ritual connected with the first layout of field systems over these lands around the 14th century BC? The site was revived and remodelled three centuries or more later, in the context of ceremonies associated with feasting that were probably still linked with the land, its productivity and perhaps continued ownership by the local Late Bronze Age community.

The characteristic elements of later Bronze Age and **Iron Age** society in Britain appears to be greater emphasis on the land and its productivity, larger and more permanent settlements, and a steadily expanding population within the context of a seemingly more egalitarian society. Despite the superiority of iron over bronze as a metal, its adoption in Britain may initially have had as much to do with growing shortages of supply as with technological superiority. Iron was more widely available and does not seem to have had been used in the same way as bronze, which was deposited as hoards of tools or weapons in rivers and pools, or as currency within systems of exchange and as expressions of prestige. There is much less emphasis now upon burial and commemoration of the dead, and the more grandiose ceremonial monuments of the later Neolithic and Early Bronze Age were perhaps neg-

Maesbury hillfort, aerial view

lected or superseded by more modest sites and expressions of ritual and religion, as at Gore End Farm. The archaeology of the first half of the first millennium BC seems to point to a more egalitarian type of society, but equally there is evidence suggesting that this may have been relatively short lived.

In the south and west of England the Iron Age is still characterised above all by those large embanked enclosures known as hillforts, often located on prominent hills and distinguished by circuits of great banks and ditches. Somerset has its fair share of hillforts, some of the most impressive examples being **South Cadbury Castle** and **Ham Hill** or **Dolebury** at the west end of Mendip. Further east are more modest but still impressive sites like **Maesbury** above Shepton Mallet, **Small Down Knoll** near Evercreech, or **Tedbury Camp** near Mells. Originally, these sites were thought of primarily as defended strongholds, perhaps the centre for a local tribe and its chief, but more recent archaeological research suggests a more complex story. Many sites have much older origins, South Cadbury in the Late Bronze Age and earlier in the Neolithic; Small Down Knoll containing an earlier Bronze Age barrow cemetery, only acquiring their more impressive defences in the last few centuries BC. Some contained little evidence of permanent settlement or of only intermittent use, while others may have been repositories for surplus grain and other crops, for livestock herding, metalworking and other industries or were centres for ritual and religion, as well as playing an occasional

South Cadbury Castle Hillfort

defensive role as refuges in times of inter-tribal strife. Whatever their different uses and histories, hillforts are probably best seen as local centres that symbolised the identity and status of local communities or tribes. This element became increasingly important as the tensions and pressures within later Iron Age society show through their increasing scale and elaboration, more evidence of warfare and the dominance of individual leaders or tribal elites.

Very few sites have been investigated, but even where relatively intensive occupation can be demonstrated, as at South Cadbury or Ham Hill, many more people would have lived in farms or small villages in the surrounding countryside. Few of these settlements were defended and their remains can be elusive, although the presence of later and more visible Roman and medieval sites can be a clue to their prehistoric forbearers. At **Ilchester**, where the Fosse Way crosses the River Yeo on its way to the South West, excavations around the town have found traces of Late Bronze Age and Iron Age settlements, and others adjacent to other nearby Roman settlements like **Catsgore** or **Podimore**. There are traces of Iron Age occupation on the Fosse Lane Roman settlement site at Shepton Mallet, and a more completely excavated farmstead was found just outside its southern boundary below the **Cannards Grave** roundabout. Here were the outlines of what had been circular, thatched and post- built timber houses, stores or work huts, along with occa-

Ditch marking the site of an Iron Age round house at Cannards Grave,
Shepton Mallet, 1996

sional pits and ditches, probably built and occupied some time between 500 BC and 300 BC.

Despite their relative rarity, some of the most spectacular and detailed surviving remains of Iron Age villages has come from excavation of the waterlogged settlements at **Glastonbury** and **Meare** on the Somerset Levels. The remains found suggests that these lakeside or platform-built settlements were of higher status than sites like Cannards Grave, as centres for trade and a broad range of manufacturing, including metal, glass, pottery, bone and textile working, with wide contacts across the South West. No less important is the evidence preserved in waterlogged conditions for their buildings, food and the more perishable items of everyday life. Its is thanks to these survivals that we can piece together such a detailed picture of everyday life in the Iron Age, as a visit to the **Peat Moors Centre** at Westhay will amply demonstrate, and help to flesh out and better interpret more sparsely preserved remains excavated on other sites.

Among the items manufactured at Glastonbury and Mere was pottery decorated in a distinctive 'celtic' style, more familiar as ornamentation on Late

Iron Age roundhouse reconstruction at The Peat Moors Centre, Westhay

Iron Age metalwork like swords, shields or mirrors. Analysis of the clays used for its manufacture demonstrated links with Devon and Cornwall, but a more local source for grit to temper the clay was **Beacon Hill**. Further links to the Mendip Hills are demonstrated by querns and various sharpening or rubber stones from the sandstones of Blackdown, Priddy, Pen Hill and, once again, Beacon Hill, whose products also reached hillforts like Cadbury Castle or Ham Hill. Not only can some stone be sourced on Beacon Hill but there is evidence still surviving for the original quarry sites within the woodland crowning the hill today. This was already a special place for earlier Bronze Age communities to bury and commemorate their dead; was this status and regard maintained by their Iron Age descendants, albeit in new ways?

Beacon Hill, Shepton Mallet from the southwest

Romano-Britons

The **Roman** conquest and annexation of large parts of Britain into a new province of its empire dates from the conquest of Claudius in A.D. 43. The process took several decades, but had been anticipated a century earlier by the expeditions of Julius Caesar and growing commercial links thereafter. Politics and prestige were probably of greater significance than economic benefit to the empire, although much of south-eastern Britain certainly prospered in the centuries to come. Initially, the conquest may have been a dramatic and sometimes catastrophic event for its inhabitants and communities, but in most places life went on again as the descendants of the Iron Age peoples of Britain adopted new ways or adapted the old, to become citizens of *Britannia* and ultimately of Rome.

These romanised Britons will always have formed the overwhelming majority of the population, encouraged to integrate with the new system and rule themselves at a local level. But a military conquest and occupation necessarily preceded this, the degree of resistance or acceptance varying between different tribes and communities. In our region it is the **Fosse Way**, which above all perhaps personifies this and the new regime. Striking south from a fort beside a crossing of the River Avon close to the hot springs at **Bath**, the road heads southwest, via what may have been another fort at **Camerton**, across

Roman soldiers: 'The Ermine Street Guard'

Roman settlement remains at Charterhouse on Mendip

the Mendip Hills by Shepton Mallet and down across the lowlands to another river crossing and fort at **Ilchester**, on its way to the coast at Seaton and eventually to **Exeter**. This is a military road, built by the army within perhaps two or three years of the conquest, though doubtless with some conscripted local labour, to help pacify the local populace and to serve the forts and army units garrisoning the South West.

Another road was built, perhaps almost at the same time, along the top of Mendip to link the mining centres at **Charterhouse** and **Priddy** ultimately with the south coast at Southampton. Lead and silver were mined here, probably before the Roman takeover, and a small fort or supply base was built at Charterhouse soon after the conquest. Direct military involvement seems to have been short-lived, but the mining and processing of metals flourished under civil operation, generating the small industrial town whose remains are still visible as earthworks within the fields around Charterhouse today. This road crosses the Fosse Way at **Beacon Hill**, just north of Shepton Mallet, although there is no evidence of a military presence there. What was there

1st century AD Roman lead ingots from Mendip lead mines

however was an outcrop of sandstone that had long been mined for querns and grinding stones, as we have seen and now proved suitable as metalling for the new roads. This was demonstrated on the earliest surface of the Fosse Way at **Shepton Mallet**, found during excavations for a new retail development at Charlton on the edge of Shepton Mallet in 2004. Here was to develop a new centre for the region, alongside the new road and dependant upon it and the Roman system of government and economy that operated in southern Britain for the next three and a half centuries or so.

Roman writers, beginning with Julius Caesar, give us glimpses of Britain and its peoples before and soon after the Claudian Conquest. These and other written sources, including inscriptions, provide an outline of the late Iron Age tribal groupings, politics and economies; a system that was largely retained and adapted to suit the new order. From these clues we know that north Somerset and the Mendip Hills were separate from the lowlands to the south and west. The latter, with **Ilchester** as their local centre, belonged within the tribal group or, in Roman terms, the *civitas* of the *Durotriges*, based ultimately on **Dorchester** in Dorset. The peoples of Mendip and further north may have been linked to or a part of the *Dobunni*, a tribe centred on the Cotswolds and lower Severn valley, although they seem later to have been incorporated within the Roman canton of the *Belgae*, based on **Winchester**.

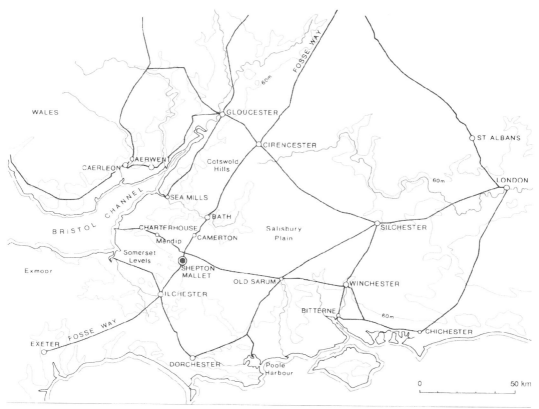

Shepton Mallet and the Fosse Way in Roman Britain

Both the *Belgae*, and, probably the *Dobunni* may have accepted the Roman takeover with little or no resistance, but their south-western neighbours were a different matter. The *Durotriges* and probably their cousins in Devon and Cornwall (the *Dumnonii*) resisted the Roman occupation. Archaeological discoveries at hillforts like **Maiden Castle** and **Hod Hill** in Dorset, or **South Cadbury Castle** and **Ham Hill** in Somerset suggest attacks and conquest by a Roman army under the command of the future emperor Vespasian. This may have resulted in a longer and more extensive military occupation of Durotrigan and Dumnonian lands, as forts at **Waddon Hill** and Hod Hill, Dorset, Ilchester, and probably within the ramparts of Ham Hill, testify. But within a generation even the legionary fortress at Exeter was abandoned as the army was needed for campaigns in Wales and the North, and southern Britain was encouraged to adopt local self government.

Its military purpose now made redundant, the Fosse Way had an important new role to play in the emerging civil province and in particular for our

The Civitates of Roman Britain

region. Towns like Winchester, Exeter or Dorchester were established early by the Roman administration as political/governmental centres for the tribal-based *civitas* regions, roughly equivalent to, if rather larger than, our modern counties. Towns and urban society on the classical Mediterranean model was new to Britain, but was an essential element in the governance of a new province and as an exemplar to its native inhabitants, encouraging them to adopt Roman ways and integrate more successfully into the imperial system. Apart from the army, the Roman occupation brought new people from all over the Empire into Britain, administrators, tax collectors, merchants and entrepreneurs, and some new landowners, but the great majority were the

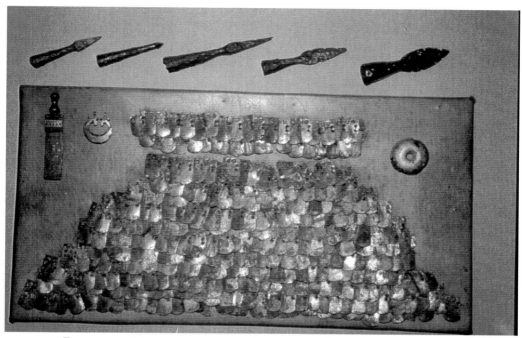

Roman military armour and weapons found on Ham Hill

native inhabitants, and it was the members of the existing aristocracy who played the major role in governance and administration of the emerging civil province.

The Great Bath showing its lead lining, Bath

The Mendip/North Somerset region was relatively remote from the *civitas* centres at Winchester or Dorchester, but roads like the Fosse Way or the Charterhouse link encouraged the local aristocracy to play their part; while closer to hand were the developing towns at **Ilchester** (*Lindinis*) and **Bath** (*Aquae Sulis*). The Roman army was quick to recognise the potential of Bath and its hot springs, and by the 2nd century the site had developed as a major religious centre and resort, in itself an important local exemplar of classical culture. Ilchester was an important commercial centre, at the head of a navigable river linking it to the Bristol Channel and a central road junction. Although of modest size, its planned street system and later defensive walls suggest an additional importance, and it may subsequently have achieved the administrative status of a *civitas* for the *Lendinienses*, a northern division of the *Durotriges* whose focus was the Somerset Moors and the rich agricultural lands of South Somerset.

As the southern parts of Britain became more integrated within the imperial Roman system there are signs of expanding agricultural land use and production, increasing rural and urban populations, exploitation of new mineral resources, new industries, and a general increase in prosperity throughout the 2nd century in particular. Our region shared in this prosperity, as local archaeological discoveries, excavations or surveys amply demonstrate.

Ilchester, aerial view from the north

Roman quern segments of Beacon Hill sandstone

The early importance of lead mining on Mendip has already been highlighted, associated with the extraction of silver, and there is every reason to suppose that this flourished through much of the Roman administration. Stone extraction on **Beacon Hill** began in prehistoric times, as we have seen, but was almost certainly expanded, to supply querns and millstones in particular to communities around the region. Many of the quarry excavations are still preserved within Beacon Wood, and recent excavations there have located at least one building that may have been occupied by quarry workers. Stone was also of growing importance for new buildings, and the quarrying of high-quality Bath stone for that town and other high-status buildings in the region began at this time. The presence of **Doulting** stone on sites closer to Mendip suggests that quarrying began here also, although no contemporary extraction or working sites have yet been found. Other stones utilized for building included Lias for walls, paving and tiles, and Pennant sandstone from the north Somerset coalfield area for roofing. The occasional presence of coal from excavated Roman sites around the region, and a notable literary allusion by the 3rd-century Roman writer Solinus to its use in the temple at Bath: *'Over these springs Minerva presides and in her temple the perpetual fire never whitens to ash, but as the flame fades, turns into rocky lumps'* suggests that there was some working of coal in the Radstock area.

Reconstructed roof of Pennant Sandstone roof tiles

Roman pottery kilns found at The Anglo Bavarian Brewery site, Shepton Mallet in 1864

Pottery production began at **Shepton Mallet** before the end of the 1st century AD. Kilns were discovered in the 19th century during the building of the Anglo Bavarian Brewery in the town. These were making bowls, mugs and tankards, mortaria for food preparation, and some flagons, made of a predominantly fine orange fabric. These styles and fabrics are more familiar in the Severn Valley around Gloucester and the location of this manufactory at Shepton Mallet is something of a mystery, being some distance away from the Fosse Way roadside settlement. The production of fine wares may not have continued there beyond the 2nd century but a range of coarser, grey table, storage and cooking vessels were probably also produced to supply the nearby small town and surrounding settlements on into the 4th century. Another centre of pottery production in the region has been identified by kiln sites around the villages of **Congresbury** and **Yatton** in north Somerset. This industry was active during the 3rd and 4th centuries, producing coarse greywares for customers located mainly north of the Mendip Hills. Other local sources of coarse pottery production probably existed around towns like Bath or Ilchester, although the larger manufacturers were usually based in the countryside, where clay, water, wood and charcoal fuel were more conveniently available. The products of potteries established around Poole Harbour dominated the supply to most settlements along the Fosse Way and

Black Burnished Ware pottery vessels

its region for much of the Roman period. Commonly known as Black Burnished ware, this industry developed early, out of the native Durotrigan potting tradition, and was soon supplying military and civilian sites all across Roman Britain.

Industry and commerce were effectively new elements in Romano-British society but its economy was overwhelmingly agricultural at the time of the conquest, and the continued prosperity of *Britannia* depended overwhelmingly upon this and its products. The permanent presence of a large army garrison for northern Britain was a major and enduring stimulus to agriculture on the one hand, along with membership and the demands of the wider Roman Empire (notably taxation!) on the other. Archaeological investigations are necessarily selective, but excavations and surveys over the past few decades in this region are increasingly demonstrating this effect and its impact on the countryside and people who lived and worked in it.

Surveys combined with small-scale excavation in areas like **Shapwick** on the Polden Hills, around South Cadbury Castle, or on the Somerset Moors and Levels suggest that the 2nd century in particular was a time of expansion or founding of new agricultural settlements, more intensive exploitation and reorganisation of existing agricultural landscapes, as well as the appearance

The Somerset moors and Brent Knoll from Compton Bishop

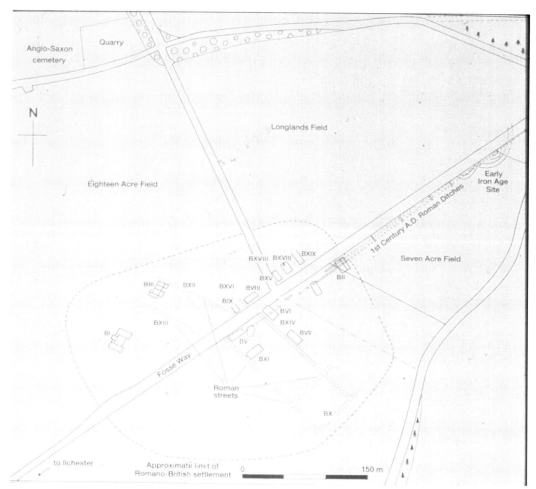

Plan of the Roman settlement at Camerton

of new crops, cultivation methods, or changes of emphasis within domestic animal husbandry. Great tracts of the moors and levels north and south of Mendip were drained for agriculture and settlement in places, doubtless contributing to the later prosperity of the region as demonstrated in the proliferation of wealthy villa estates. Some of these landscapes of fields and farms still survive as surface traces in areas like the **Axe valley** between Wookey and Cheddar, or on the moors north of **Banwell**. Relatively few agricultural settlements have been investigated further east towards the Fosse Way, although ongoing excavations at **Blacklands,** Hemington near Frome have demonstrated the unusually early development of a villa estate there from its native Iron Age origins.

Developments closer to the road have more often been the subject of archaeological exploration, with the urban centres of Bath and Ilchester the principal foci, but the Fosse Way itself was a focus for further settlement. One of the earliest to be recognised and excavated was at **Camerton**, between Radstock and Bath. Camerton's origin may lie in its apparent status as a late Iron Age political/religious local centre, that may then have been the location for a fort of the conquest period. It subsequently developed as a roadside village or small town, with side streets, stone and timber-framed buildings, one or two villa-style buildings and a possible shrine. The settlement flourished until at least the 4th century and there is evidence for the production of pewter vessels in workshops on the site. A few miles further down the road are remains of what may have been another village-type settlement at **Downside**, Stretton-on-the-Fosse, where several stone buildings have been identified, although little is known of its origin, function, or full extent.

Fosse Lane

Almost midway between Bath and Ilchester lies the more extensive and better explored settlement at **Fosse Lane**, Charlton, on the eastern fringe of Shepton Mallet. We have already seen that prehistoric farming communities were attracted here, utilising and sometimes settling in the locality from at least the beginning of the third millennium BC. Finds from sites on Fosse Lane hint at some Iron Age occupation, as distinct from the farm site near Cannards Grave, but whether this was present or indeed displaced by construction of the Fosse Way in the mid or late 40s AD is unclear. Did the army build a fort in the locality at this time? There is no evidence of this at the Beacon Hill road crossing to the north, nor from any remains of lost equipment or structures at Fosse Lane. The early manufacture of pottery at Shepton Mallet might have been a direct response to the military as a supplier, although it could have begun slightly later and there is no other evidence of the army at the kiln sites.

The Fosse Way and Fosse Lane Roman settlement excavation, 1990, view north

We may never know exactly how or why the Fosse Lane settlement originated, although one major factor may have been the will and initiative of the local native aristocracy. They and their inheritors probably continued to

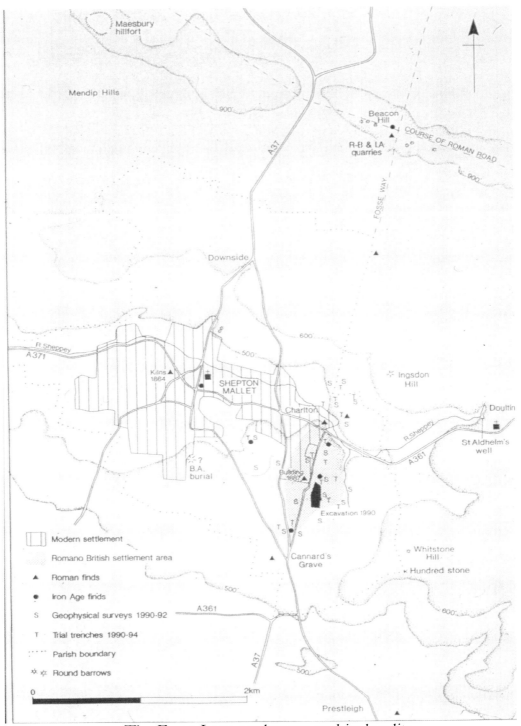

The Fosse Lane settlement and its locality

Lead coffin burial found at Fosse Lane in 1988

have title to the land under the Roman system and may have seen a commercial opportunity here. The settlement lies on one of the major trunk roads of Roman Britain with its links to the South West; almost mid-way between Bath and Ilchester, but also close to the border between two *civitates* - just within that of the *Belgae* (or *Dobunni?*), with the *Durotriges* to the south.

Effectively, the Fosse Lane settlement was virtually unknown until 1990, when the modern expansion of Shepton Mallet resulted in a series of excavations and surveys that have continued into the 21st century to reveal its true extent and character. The first clue to its existence was the discovery of a substantial stone building during construction of a branch line of the Somerset and Dorset Railway to Shepton Mallet in 1887. In the 1980s discoveries by metal detectorists in fields along the east side of Fosse Lane resulted in the excavation of a lead coffin and hinted at a more extensive settlement. This was finally proven by large scale excavations on a site then owned by Showerings for a new warehouse, subsequently by surveys and

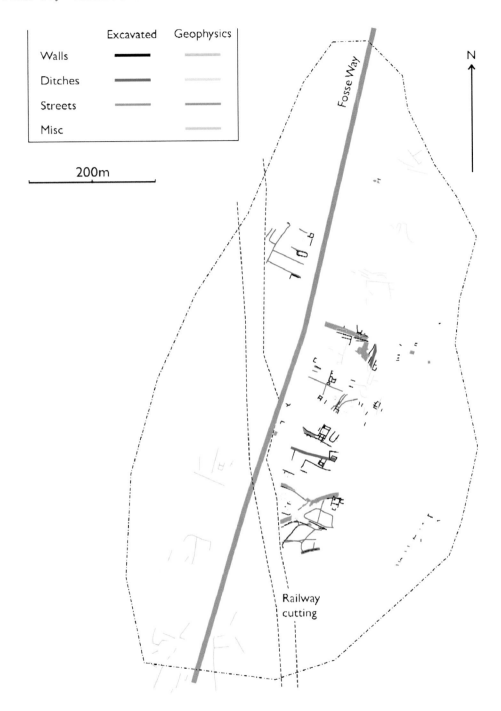

Archaeological remains, Fosse Lane settlement site

excavations on development sites within the adjacent Mendip Business Park, and more recently on the site of a Focus retail store development on the west side of Fosse Lane. Progressively, these discoveries have built up a picture of a small roadside town extending south for almost 1km along the road between its crossing of the River Sheppy to the Cannards Grave roundabout. Covering some 30 hectares, the best preserved remains now survive at its southern end, where they are further protected under pasture as a scheduled Ancient Monument. Local Authority planning conditions have ensured that most of the post-1990 developments include provision for archaeological excavation or protection through burial of most areas elsewhere within the settlement site, and a programme of detailed academic analysis and publication of the remains is ongoing.

A great deal of the information collected through this programme of excavation and survey across the site relates to its later history and development, but glimpses of remains dating to the earliest periods provide clues to the origin of the settlement. One of the first acts may have been to lay out a series of plots or enclosures alongside the Fosse Way, which were defined by ditched or stone-walled boundaries. Some of these layouts are still visible within later arrangements and development of the settlement and probably determined

Building remains west of the Fosse Way, 2004, Fosse Lane settlement

its general character thereafter. These plots were effectively properties, occupied by an owner or tenant, within which a variety of activities took place.
Original control or ownership of the land was probably in the hands of the
local aristocracy, who could have leased out plots to individuals or laid them
out in advance. Very few areas of the road frontages have been available for
excavation, although on one of the few areas excavated west of the road in
2004 at least three fairly regular, rectangular plots, defined originally by
ditches, seem to have been laid out together. The settlement was more extensive to the east and plots of more variable size and shape are found, although
it has nowhere been possible to investigate the eastern road frontage. Despite
this there are signs of regularity and thus some deliberate planning in sets of
elongated plot layouts.

We may never know who was responsible for founding the town, who its
inhabitants were and what their status was, although we can be almost cer-
tain that the great majority will have been native British people and mostly of
local origin. However, thanks to the extensive and widespread opportunities
for excavation we do have plenty of archaeological evidence for what they
were doing, how and where they lived or were buried, and the history of their
town.

Excavating plots and boundaries, Fosse Lane settlement, 1990

Apart from hints of some late Iron Age settlement, the earliest remains are pottery types, bronze brooches and rare coins, that date from the last few decades of the 1st century AD. Some of these finds have come from boundary ditches or pits belonging to the initial layout of properties and their occupation, but contemporary buildings or other structures have been more difficult to identify. This is partly due to the rarity of opportunities to excavate close to the frontages alongside the Fosse Way, but also because sites in those locations were occupied successively over several centuries. This has probably obliterated remains of the earliest buildings, most of which would probably have been timber built.

As the settlement became established and grew during the 2nd century AD a clearer picture of its layout and character emerges. This process was enhanced by the widespread adoption of stone, which has aided the preservation and recognition of many more structures. The settlement is founded upon formations of the Upper Lias limestone of Jurassic age; a hard, well-bedded, grey-white limestone ideal for building and easily available close to the surface. This and the presence of other stone types nearby, along with the Roman introduction of mortar and cement, must have quickly transformed its appearance. Finer building detail could be provided using stone from

A side street in the Fosse Lane settlement, 1996

nearby Doulting or Downside, Shepton Mallet, while some Lias limestone formations on the nearby Polden Hills can be split to provide stone for paving or roof tiles. Stone was also used widely to define property boundaries. Drystone walls replaced some of the original banks and ditches and were used to lay out new plots, especially on the east side of the road, where parts of the settlement extend up to 300m back from the road as far as the small stream alongside Frog Lane, Charlton.

Thanks to the opportunities for exposure of quite extensive areas of the eastern part of the Fosse Lane settlement we have a relatively complex picture of plots and enclosures of varying shape and size, changing over time, containing a variety of buildings and other structures relating to their use, and served in places by side streets or lanes. One of the most substantial streets, found on the site of a Tesco retail development in 1996, was almost 8m wide and built of successive gravel, stone cobble and compacted clay layers over 0.5m thick. This may have been laid out, along with a set of elongated properties at right angles to the Fosse Way, early in the 2nd century. They were subsequently affected by local flooding, but continued in use as a street through to at least the later 4th century. Another street of similar width found in 1990 curved between several plots further south, its cobbled surface sometimes encroached upon by later buildings.

Excavating Building VII, Fosse Lane settlement, 1990

Recording evidence of burning, Building VII, Fosse Lane, settlement, 1990

It is unfortunate that we have so little knowledge of buildings fronting the east side of the main road, but several substantial mortared stone buildings have been identified within properties further back that were built during the 2nd century. One of the best preserved was found in 1990 on the former Showerings site, whose remains had survived paradoxically through a fire that led to its collapse or demolition. This was a rectangular house (Building VII), 13m by 8m in area and divided into three ground-floor rooms. The two smallest at the south end were a kitchen with hearths and ovens, and a smaller store room which still contained several pottery jars. The remainder of the building comprised a large room with a cobbled floor, while its very substantial foundation walls suggest the likelihood of an upper storey of rooms. The fire may have started in the kitchen, where the carbonised wood doorsills were found still in position beneath collapsed debris. At least two other rectangular buildings of this type with two or three ground-floor rooms were found further north in 1996 but not so thoroughly excavated. Part of another 2nd-century stone building with a semicircular apse was also found in 1990, possibly to be replaced in the 4th century by Building I, but it was not fully excavated.

Another style of stone-founded building that originated in the 2nd century

Aerial view of Buildings VII, VIII, IX & X, Fosse Lane settlement, 1990

was an elongated structure, over 16m long and 8m wide with rounded corners in this area (Building X). Internal dividing walls indicated several rooms with cobbled or paved floors, although the whole structure was not exposed. Spreads of burnt pottery, stone and carbonised grain beneath rubble within one room suggest that this building may also have suffered a fire. In 2004 excavation on the west side of the Fosse Way revealed the foundations of three more buildings of this type, two of which were excavated fairly thoroughly. These fronted on to the main road and were set at the corners of larger plots approximately 30m wide, which separated the buildings. The plots contained evidence of more ephemeral outbuildings, and structures including hearths and ovens, pits, drains and pathways. The buildings themselves continued in use until at least the 4th century, probably functioning as combinations of residence, shops and workshops, although it is difficult to know the exact nature of their business. This type of building might have resembled a medieval longhouse, housing a variety of activities that could even include some animals, and were possibly of half-timbered construction with a thatched roof.

The establishments found in 2004 are closely linked with the working life and economy of the Fosse Lane settlement, and may have been located within a

Excavations on the west road frontage Fosse Lane settlement, 2004

semi-industrial zone here. Further south, however, there were more ambitious buildings on this side of the road. In 1887 construction of the Somerset and Dorset railway revealed the remains of a very substantial stone house close to the entrance of what is now a small industrial estate on the west side of Fosse Lane. Unfortunately this was destroyed in the process, and although finds of pottery, coins, metalwork, etc were recovered, and some details of its construction recorded, we have no plan of its layout. From what was recovered and recorded this was evidently a building of some status, possibly equivalent to a villa, and certainly in occupation during the 4th century. Other major stone buildings are hinted at further south in the fields towards the Cannards Grave roundabout (now protected as a Scheduled Ancient Monument), through geophysical survey and glimpsed within a water main trench cut across this area in 1996.

The clearest evidence of later Roman buildings comes from excavations on the east side of the road. One of the most ambitious was found in 1990 (Building IX), in total around 25m long and over 10m wide, comprising a central aisled hall or courtyard with a suite of rooms at the south end that may have had upper floors, and another room or vestibule added at the north end. There was evidence of plaster and plaster interior walls, window glass,

Reconstruction of Building IX, Fosse Lane settlement

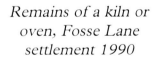

Remains of a kiln or oven, Fosse Lane settlement 1990

stone flagged or cobbled floors, and stone tiles for roofing, but no sign of the tessellated mosaic floors or underfloor heating found in wealthier villa build-ings. This building lay close to the 2nd century Buildings VII and X, possibly replacing the latter and was in occupation during the 4th century. Another of similar ground plan and date lay to the south (Building I), which may also have been replacing a predecessor incompletely explored to the east. At least one other large rectangular building occupied during the 4th century was located on the former Tesco development site in 1996. Comprising a suite of six ground-floor rooms, this building had some painted plaster walls but has been left mainly unexcavated beneath what is now the car park.

The remains of mortared stone buildings of this type inevitably stand out, but these were by no means the only structures found. Several more were detected through the outline of their paved or cobbled floors and sometimes by postholes or shallow gullies; clues to the sites of suspected timber-framed buildings. These were mostly of rectangular form though usually smaller and of simpler plan than the stone buildings. Some of these housed or were asso-ciated with industrial features, notably hearths, ovens or kilns, which were found widely across the settlement. One of these ovens found in 1990 was set within a small rectangular building with partial stone foundations close to the demolished Building VII that may have been a smithy (Building VIII). Another further west may have been for smelting or processing lead; an ingot

4th-century lead ingot with producers name 'MINNIUS',
Fosse Lane settlement, 1990

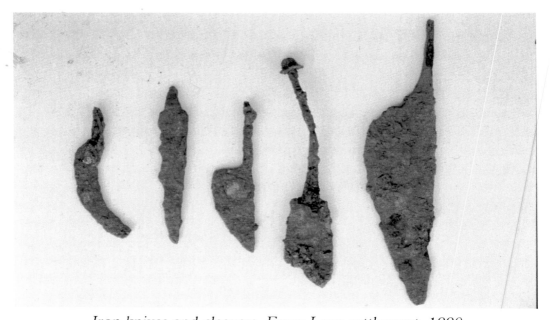

Iron knives and cleavers, Fosse Lane settlement, 1990

with the name stamp 'MINNIUS' denoting its owner or producer was found alongside the oven, probably a product of the Mendip lead-mining industry. Others may have been used for cooking or bread-making, and at least one set into the northern room of Building IX was probably a grain-malting oven. Burnt wheat was found on the floor of Building X, and many fragments and occasional complete querns and millstones for grinding corn have been found across the settlement.

Evidence for other activities and occupations of the inhabitants found within the property enclosures can be less easy to identify. Leather tanning and processing, as well as spinning, weaving and dyeing of wool is suggested by pits and drainage channels, as well as tools of bone or iron used in such processes. A large stone-lined pit found in one of the buildings west of the Fosse Way in 2004 might have been for tanning or dyeing. Live animals were also brought into the settlement for consumption, but perhaps also to be marketed. The animal bones found suggest a disproportionate number of older individuals among sheep and cattle, while the evidence of butchery on their bones is backed up by finds of iron knives, cleavers and flesh hooks from the site. Some of the enclosures may have been used as paddocks for animals, notably where there is little or no evidence of other activities. Part of one plot examined in 1996 contained at least two large stone-lined cisterns

Stone lined water conduit, Fosse Lane settlement, 1996

fed by stone drains, probably for watering animals, but was otherwise almost vacant.

There is no suggestion that the Fosse Lane settlement ever had any particular status, beyond its evident function as a small rural market and commercial/industrial centre serving its region. Regrettably we have no record of its Roman name, and there is no sign that it was ever formally enclosed by walls or embankments, although there appears to have been a long-standing and well-demarcated southern boundary to the settlement towards Cannards Grave where the Fosse Way entered. It is unlikely to have had any public buildings like a bathhouse or basilica, and no church or temple has been found, although one or more of these might be expected.

A number of pagan temples in rural settings are known in Somerset, which were developed and flourishing particularly well in the 4th century. Several have been excavated, including one on **Brean Down** at the western extremity of Mendip, one at **Henley Wood**, Yatton, one at **Pagans Hill** overlooking the Chew Valley, and, closer to Fosse Lane, on the summit of **Lamyatt Beacon** near Evercreech. This last site was extensively damaged by 20th-century treasure hunters but enough survived to reveal a classic square Romano-Celtic building comprising an inner room or sanctum with surrounding

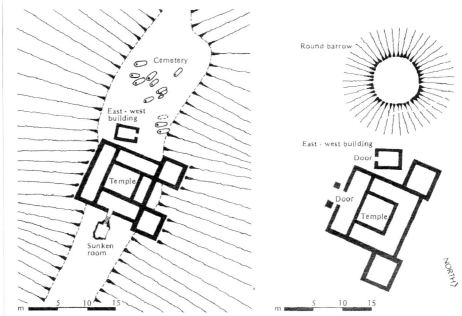

*Plans of Romano-Celtic temples at Lamyatt Beacon (left)
and Brean Down (right)*

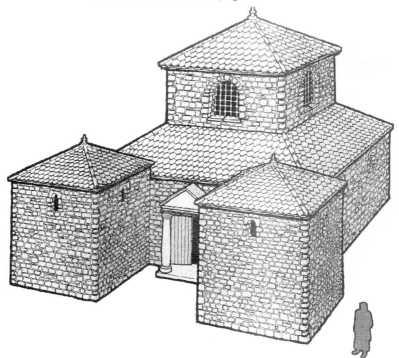

Reconstruction of the main temple building at Lamyatt Beacon

Lamyatt Beacon and Creech Hill from the north

ambulatory or corridor and some additional rooms. Stone statuary and metal figurines, among other finds, suggest that a range of classical deities were worshipped, including Mars, Jupiter, Mercury and Minerva, while votive

Roman coins from the Fosse Lane settlement

Enamelled bronze brooch, Fosse Lane settlement, 2004

offerings are represented by miniature pottery vessels, jewellery and numerous coins. This site may have had a prehistoric sanctity, and might well have been frequented by the citizens of Fosse Lane. It seems to have been partly demolished around the end of the 4th century, and the subsequent presence of a small rectangular, east west aligned building and a small group of early post-Roman burials raise the possibility that it then became the site of an early Christian oratory or hermitage in the 5th or 6th centuries.

Whatever its exact status the inhabitants of Fosse Lane seem to have prospered, adopting much of the culture and life-style of the most romanised inhabitants of the province. Its local market functions apart, the settlement was operating within a money economy, as relatively plentiful quantities of coin finds from the site demonstrate. The Romans introduced taxation to Britain and it is possible that its local collection could have been organised here. Coinage became more widely used in the 3rd and 4th centuries with issues of lower value, their loss demonstrating that the settlement was probably still flourishing to the end of the 4th century. Its prosperity is also demonstrable through the possessions of its inhabitants. These have included finds of brooches, rings, earrings and dress fittings, as well as items such as furniture fittings, keys, writing styli, combs, gaming pieces, and toilette or medical instruments, usually of bronze or bone but occasionally in silver. None of the textiles, wooden or other organic-based items have survived, but

Finger rings; silver(left), bronze with glass intaglio (right),
Fosse Lane settlement

more durable are ceramics; pottery above all. Most Roman settlement sites are characterised and initially identified by an abundance of pottery, providing information on local economies, occupations, life-styles and the communities' wider contacts.

Fosse Lane was evidently being supplied at an early date from its own local industry, the Shepton Mallet kilns, with relatively fine bowls, mortaria, flagons and tankards of a pink-orange fabric. Later its products were predominantly coarser grey fabrics for cooking, storage and some table ware. Almost as common was Black Burnished Ware from the Poole Harbour area of Dorset in a similar range of cooking, storage and table wares, which was exported widely across Roman Britain. Less common imports were finer table and cooking wares from the Oxfordshire or New Forest industrial manufacturing centres, appearing particularly during the 4th century. Much rarer are imports from further afield; fine tablewares from France and the Rhineland, especially glossy red-slipped Samian ware, and the amphorae which brought wine or oil (mostly from Spain), which were often then reused as storage containers.

For the Roman West Country in particular the 4th century seems to have

Beakers and flasks made in the New Forest potteries

Mid-2nd century Samian bowl

been a time of considerable prosperity. This is epitomised above all perhaps by the development of villas and their estates, reflecting the wealth and status of their owners and rooted essentially in the strength of the local agricultural economy by that time. One of the densest concentrations of villas known in Britain was around Ilchester, with the concentration around Bath a close second. The grandest of these houses were graced by elaborate baths and suites of living and reception rooms, underfloor heating, gardens, and rooms decorated with sophisticated mosaic floors and painted walls or ceilings. At **Pitney** near Somerton was a pavement depicting the Four Seasons, while from nearby **Low Ham** comes the pavement with scenes from Virgil's Aeneid displayed in the County Museum at Taunton. No such concentration is known close to Fosse Lane, the nearest identified sites lying mainly to the north, including **Holcombe**, **Wellow** and **Whatley**, which had pavements featuring Orpheus and the goddess Cybele. A finely modelled bronze figurine of a *lar* (a household god) from **Castle Cary** may have come from another villa there. More modest villa-type buildings have been found at **Chew Park**, now beneath the Chew Valley reservoir, on the edge of the **Camerton** settlement, and probably near **Priddy**; while it is possible that another building of this type existed within the Fosse Lane settlement. An apparent scarcity of local villas however, could reflect the relative distance of the small town from political centres like Bath or Ilchester, as well as its close proximity to the boundary between two different *civitates.*

Reconstruction of the Pitney Roman villa near Somerton

Hunting scene on a 4th-century Roman villa at East Coker, near Yeovil

*Bronze figurine of a
'Lar' - a household
god - from
Castle Cary*

Rome brought Britain into the historic era, giving us some account of events and people that shaped those times, albeit with many gaps. Locally, we are fortunate if even names of places or people survive, and are dependant on archaeology to give us any meaningful picture of life in places like Fosse Lane. So far we have been unable to identify a name for the settlement, or the names of any of its inhabitants, but some of their remains have survived through burials. Methods of human burial have varied over time. Very few burials of the prehistoric Iron Age have been recognised in Somerset or more widely in Britain, although cremation and other methods of disposal that have left no trace of the body is likely for the majority of people. Cremation was certainly the usual rite during the earlier years of the Roman empire, but inhumation became the norm in the 3rd and 4th centuries. Many cremations were probably deposited or dispersed without trace, as can occur today, but where the remains were placed within a container, sometimes with other objects, they are easier to recognise.

At Fosse Lane discoveries of cremation burials have been relatively rare, though widely scattered across the settlement. One unusual example was found on the site of the Tesco development in 1996, where a small lead box or casket was buried within the primary boundary bank of one enclosure

Excavating graves in the early Christian cemetery,
Fosse Lane settlement, 1990

Burials next to Building I, Fosse Lane settlement, 1990

with a pipe that connected it to the surface. Burials of this type probably enabled the mourners to communicate with or supply libation offerings to the deceased. A few cremations have been found within pottery jars, once again buried within the remains of enclosure boundaries or beneath the floors of buildings or yards. These associations with boundaries or buildings may have significance in the context of family ancestral claims or ownership of a property. Burial within Roman towns was normally prohibited and most people were buried in cemeteries located alongside major roads leading out of town. This was the pattern at Ilchester and Bath, where large cemeteries have been found beside the Fosse Way outside both towns, but at smaller settlements like Fosse Lane things were evidently less formal.

Several inhumation burial groups have been found, along with more isolated graves, scattered widely around the settlement. Many of these seem to have a more direct association with individual properties rather than be communal burial areas, although there could be some yet to be discovered alongside the Fosse Way north or south of the town. One of the best associations with a property was found in the 1990 excavations, as a small cemetery located immediately to the west of a large stone building (Building I) within a triangular enclosure, whose boundary incorporated one of the earlier cremations

Doulting stone coffin, Building I mausoleum burial,
Fosse Lane settlement,

in a pottery jar. Notable was the burial of a young man within a stone coffin that had been fashioned reusing stone from the door casement of an earlier building, and was surrounded by a small rectangular platform which probably outlines the site of a mausoleum built above the grave. Another grave nearby for an older man contained a roughly made lead coffin with evidence of a wooden lid, and from which a radiocarbon date suggested burial in the 5th or even the 6th century. Several other burials in this cemetery were simply laid in shallow rock-cut graves. Some, if not all these burials were of post-Roman date, and there was evidence for demolition and a remodelling of the adjacent 4th-century building that indicates its later use and re-occupation.

A larger burial group within a neighbouring enclosure to the south were distinguished by their broadly east-west orientation and the inclusion of another lead coffin containing the remains of a young woman, the discovery of which in 1988 was an early clue to the significance and location of the settlement as a whole. Some of these graves contained iron nails as evidence of former wooden coffins, and one contained a unique silver amulet with a Christian cross symbol, hailed at the time of its discovery as evidence for one of the earliest Christian burials in Britain. Subsequently however, analysis of its metal composition cast doubt upon its authenticity, and more recent

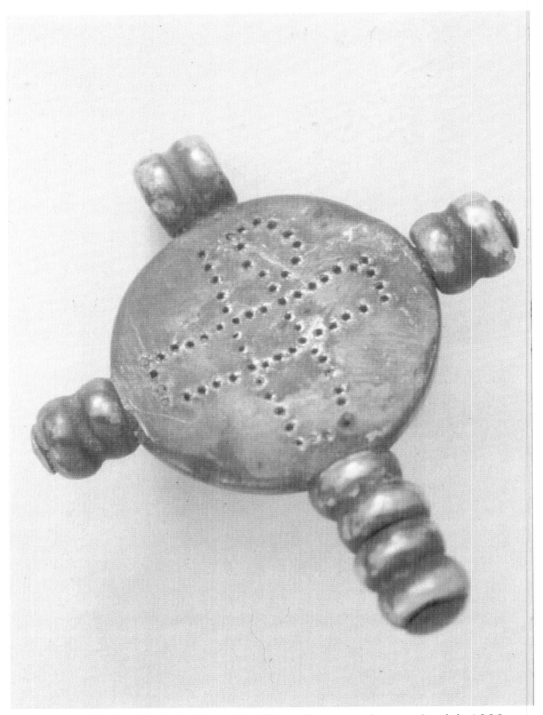

Silver "Early Christian" amulet, Fosse Lane settlement burial, 1990

analyses demonstrate that silver of this purity could not have been produced before the 19th century, suggesting that this object is now almost certainly a modern fake. All this brought the amulet to public attention again in 2008, and speculation as to how and why such an object came to be made and buried. Despite its careful excavation from within an apparently undisturbed burial deposit, the circumstances of its discovery in a grave whose excavation had begun the previous day, on an easily accessible site with low level security, and from a mixed grave fill whose disturbance could have been readily disguised, provide support for doubts about its ancient origin. Perhaps of even more interest are the motives that lie behind its creation and deposition, for which we may never have an answer. However, the discoveries along Fosse Lane in 1990 aroused enormous local and national interest, and not a little opposition to the development that led to the discovery of the Roman settlement remains. Might this have stimulated the production of an intelligent and initially convincing fake, whose discovery could influence the impending development or fate of the remains thereafter?

Whatever the truth behind the amulet, the east west grave layouts, some cut into the remains of earlier demolished structures, finds, and some radiocarbon dates suggesting 4th/5th century remains, still support the suggestion that this was a late Roman cemetery specifically for Christian burial. A further burial group on the opposite side of a side street within another

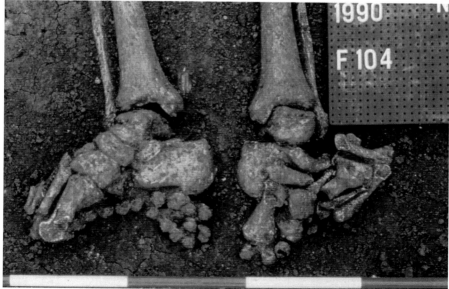

Iron hobnails at the feet of a late Roman burial,
Fosse Lane settlement, 1990

4th-century childs' burial in a Doulting stone coffin,
Fosse Lane settlement, 1996

enclosure to the west had features with pagan attributes. These more disparate burials included examples incorporating broken pottery vessels, animal bones representing food, one accompanied by a pair of hobnail boots, and body orientations broadly north south. At least two graves were set within the remains of earlier building foundations, some contained finds datable to the 4th century, while a radiocarbon date from another suggested burial in the 5th or 6th century; all of which suggests a small cemetery of late or early post-Roman date.

Elsewhere across the settlement small groups of burials have come to light wherever sufficiently extensive excavations have taken place. Thus, on the former Tesco site in 1996, a small group of graves were excavated within the enclosure from whose adjacent eastern boundary was recovered the lead cremation burial casket. One of these was a small stone coffin containing the remains of a child, which is currently displayed at the Tourist Information Office in Shepton Mallet. Another scattered group of shallow burials nearby were cut into the remains of earlier buildings or yard surfaces. More recently, excavations on the north side of Mendip Avenue in 2004 demonstrated a

Aerial view of excavation sites west (left) and east (right) of Fosse Lane, 2004

similar sequence, with graves cutting earlier boundaries or building remains that probably date them to the 4th century and later. West of the Fosse Way, excavations on the site of the Focus retail store located burials associated with plot boundaries to the rear of the road frontage buildings. Once again, the bulk of these appear to be of late or post-Roman date, and one grave was notable as a double burial, the upper in a disarticulated condition suggesting its disturbance to insert the lower body.

Many of the inhumation burials found among the remains of the Fosse Lane settlement are evidently quite late in the sequence of occupation there; some are demonstrably of early post-Roman date. What then was the fate of this settlement following Rome's abandonment of her British provinces early in the 5th century?

After Rome

The formal end of Roman Britain probably came in or around AD 410, with a letter from the Emperor Honorious to the cities (or *civitates*) of Britain to look to their own defence. This came at a time of particular pressure on the Empire as a whole from 'barbarian' peoples outside its borders, some of which was also affecting Britain. However, this picture of invasion and collapse is not the whole story. The empire had been in decline since at least the middle of the 4th century, politically and economically, the effects of which were felt especially in the western provinces. Britain was certainly under pressure from outsiders like the Saxons, Picts or Irish, who raided its shores, but it also suffered through military revolts by its garrison, led by generals with wider imperial ambitions. The latest of these attempted coups, by Magnus Maximus in 383 and Constantine III from 406, seriously depleted its resident garrisons, forcing the local *civitas* governments to look increasingly to their own defence and administration. With the defeat of Constantine III in France in 411 the final link with Rome was broken and Britain was independent once again.

Sunset over South Cadbury Castle

Our sources for this period of British history are much less informative or reliable than for the early Roman period, and even archaeological evidence declines rapidly in quantity and quality as we move into the 5th century. As the links with the empire were severed so went the imperial administration and armies, taxation and much of the extensive system of trade, and with it such things as coinage, large-scale manufacturing and marketing, and even the construction or maintenance of mortared stone buildings and the road system.

The picture of Anglo-Saxon invaders rapidly overwhelming the province can no longer be sustained. More likely was local British self-determination and government based initially upon the Romano-British *civitates* system, which probably evolved into the sub-kingdoms like those in Wales, or South West England (*Dumnonia*) that become more visible a century or so later. In many respects much of Britain may have reverted to the tribal-based system that the Romans found and adapted at the time of their conquest. Some of these states were indeed quickly overwhelmed or taken over by an Anglo-Saxon ruling class, many of whom were probably invited in initially, and which later evolved into kingdoms such as Kent, Wessex, Mercia or East Anglia. We may never have a clear picture of the early political evolution of the West Country,

Remains of post-Roman structures over Building I,
Fosse Lane settlement, 1990

Post-Roman shallow burial near building remains west of the Fosse Way, Fosse Lane settlement, 2004

although it was well into the 7th century before the kingdom of Wessex over-ran most of Somerset, while the Dumnonians of Cornwall remained inde-pendent until their final conquest in 832.

Unlike many Roman towns the settlement at Fosse Lane had no direct modern successor, which is why its existence was unknown for so long. Much of our knowledge today has come through the expansion of neighbouring Shepton Mallet, but what happened here when Roman rule gave way again to that of the native British? We have already seen that burials were continuing within the settlement through the 5th and probably into the 6th century. These alone imply a living community of some sort, among whom were perhaps those with both Christian and pagan beliefs. Other evidence comes from buildings, some of which look to have been modified in the last stages of their existence, utilising components from earlier demolished structures, or through replacement with wood. One of the clearest examples was Building I excavated in 1990 with its accompanying late and post-Roman cemetery, mentioned above. There was clear evidence for reconstruction of the original 4th-century stone building with the reuse of stones from other buildings for floors or timber footings, along with timber postholes, and the insertion of hearths and ovens into some of the earlier rooms. Several other ovens and hearths have been recognised across the settlement, apparently replacing or set within the remains of earlier structures. Reliable dates for activity of this kind is normally difficult to come by but in 2004 thermolumi-

The southwest gate of South Cadbury Castle,
refortified in the 5th-6th centuries AD.

nescent dates in the 6th century were obtained from three small hearths overlying earlier building remains on the west side of the Fosse Way.

Archaeological evidence of burials, industrial/domestic activities, or new buildings hint at life continuing for perhaps two centuries or more beyond the end of Roman rule, but gives us limited help in understanding its scale, economic, political or social basis. Fosse Lane could no longer function as a small commercial market town within a much larger provincial and imperial system. At best it may have survived as a local farming community with some additional semi-industrial and marketing role, probably owing allegiance to a local magnate or land-owning aristocrat. We know even less about its political position. Was it part of a sub-kingdom based at Bath, whose king was allegedly defeated by the West Saxons at the Battle of Dyrham in 577? Or did it look south as part of a Durotrigian sub-kingdom, one of whose strongholds was South Cadbury Castle, refortified in the 5th and 6th centuries? This part of Somerset continued under British rule until 658, when their defeat by the West Saxons at the Battle of Penselwood on the Wiltshire border must have brought the area finally into the expanding Anglo-Saxon kingdom of Wessex.

Our understanding of this shadowy period between the end of Roman rule and the 7th century Anglo-Saxon takeover - sometimes referred to as the Dark Ages - is hampered by the virtual absence of reliable textual sources and a paucity of attributable and dated archaeological remains. One of the major structures claimed for this period is the **West Wansdyke**, a bank and ditch-defined earthwork, which could have been built to separate a south western British kingdom from another centred on the Severn Valley. This boundary can be traced from **Maes Knoll** hillfort south of Bristol eastwards to another hillfort at **Stantonbury**, crossing the Fosse Way between Camerton and Bath, and may have been continued further east as the **Wansdyke** across the north Wiltshire downs.

Further glimpses of this post-Roman southwestern British community are provided by their burials - those at Fosse Lane comparable with a larger contemporary group of cemeteries identified particulary in Somerset - including those at **Henley Wood**, Congresbury, **Brean Down, Cannington** near Bridgwater, **Carhampton** near Dunster, or **Lamyatt Beacon**. Henley Wood and probably Cannington are associated with contemporary settlements within adjacent refortified iron age hillforts; Carhampton, Brean Down, and Lamyatt Beacon are associated with suspected Christian - possibly early monastic sites. The last two may have had oratories or small eremitic monastic communities, successors to demolished Roman temples; while another apparently occupied the summit of **Glastonbury Tor**. One other cultural indicator of this time was the appearance of eastern Mediterranean pottery dateable to the later 5th and 6th centuries, which has been found at most of these sites as well as the fortified centre at South Cadbury, though not at Lamyatt or Fosse Lane. This material could signify links with the emerging Byzantine empire, successor to Rome in the east. Intensive study of the South Cadbury region suggests that it may have been the focus of a large estate, which was broken up into smaller estates and parishes in late Saxon and medieval times. Might not Fosse Lane have been the centre of another?; echoes of which could be the Anglo Saxon Hundred of Whitstone and the later parish of Shepton Mallet, whose boundary crosses the line of the Fosse Way to include Charlton and the former Roman settlement site.

Further Reading

References to literature or other sources of information have not normally been included within the main text but there are many published sources, both academic and of a more popular nature that may be consulted, relating to the locality and its wider context, as suggested here.

General

General books on Somerset and local archaeology include three county surveys: Dobson, D. 1931. *The Archaeology of Somerset* (London 1931); Aston, M. and Burrow, I. (eds.) 1982. *The Archaeology of Somerset* (Somerset County Council); and Webster, C. and Mayberry, T. (eds.) 2007. *The Archaeology of Somerset* (Somerset Books); and a more wide ranging study: Costen, M. 1992. *The Origins of Somerset* (Manchester University).

The county features prominently in a recent regional research assessment: Webster, C. (ed.) 2008 *The Archaeology of South West England* (Somerset County Council); a selection of recent work is reviewed in Webster, C. (ed.) 2000. *Somerset Archaeology* (Somerset County Council); many of Somerset's historic landscapes and monuments feature in Croft, R. and Aston, M. 1993. *Somerset from the air* (Somerset County Council); and a useful handbook is: L. & R. Adkins, 1992. *A Field Guide to Somerset Archaeology* (Dovecote Press).

Of more local relevance are: Stokes, P. 1999. *Mendip's past: A Shared Inheritance* (Somerset Books); Firth, H. 2007. *Mendip from the Air. A Changing Landscape* (Somerset County Council); Williams, R. & R. 1996. *The Mendips* (Ex Libris Press) and Lewis, J. (ed.) in press *The Archaeology of Mendip* (University of Worcester).

Other regional surveys include: Riley, H. and Wilson-North, R. 2001. *The Field Archaeology of Exmoor* (English Heritage); Riley, H. 2006. *The Historic Landscape of the Quantock Hills* (English Heritage); and an equivalent survey of Mendip currently underway by English Heritage may be published similarly in the future.

Recent publication of more intensive local archaeological surveys are: Gerrard, C. and Aston, M. 2008. *The Shapwick Project, Somerset: A Rural Landscape Explored* (Society for Medieval Archaeology), and Tabor, R. 2008. *Cadbury Castle: The Hillfort and Landscapes* (Stroud).

Prehistoric archaeology

One of the best and most accessible introductions to our Palaeolithic ancestors is by Chris Stringer 2006. *Homo Britannicus* (Allen Lane); one other with a more local emphasis is Barham, L. 1999. *In Search of Cheddar Man* (Tempus). Later prehistoric archaeology is covered by many of the publications listed above, to which might be added Bradley, R. 2007. *The Prehistory of Britain and Ireland* (Cambridge University Press), Darvill, T. 1987. *Prehistoric Britain* (Routledge); or Prior, F. 2003. *Britain BC* (Harper Collins).

More detailed and local to Somerset are: Barrett, J., Freeman, P. & Woodward, A. 2000. *Cadbury Castle, Somerset: The Later Prehistoric and Early Historic Archaeology* (English Heritage); Bell, M. 1990. *Brean Down Excavations* 1983-1987 (English Heritage); Coles, B. and J. 1986. *Sweet Track to Glastonbury: The Somerset Levels in Prehistory* (Thames and Hudson); or Coles, J. & Minnitt, S. 1995 *'Industrious and fairly civilized' The Glastonbury Lake Village* (Somerset County Museum). Many more detailed and site-specific publications are to be found in the pages of the *Proceedings of the Somerset Archaeological and Natural History Society* (Taunton), or the *Proceedings of the University of Bristol Spelaeological Society* (Bristol).

Roman and later archaeology

Good introductions to these periods are Frere, S. 1987. *Britannia* (Routledge); Salway, P. 1993. *The Oxford Illustrated History of Roman Britain* (Oxford); Millet, M. 1990. *The Romanization of Britain* (Cambridge); Esmonde Cleary, S. 1989. *The Ending of Roman Britain* (Batsford); or Dark, K. 2000. *Britain and the end of the Roman Empire* (Tempus).

Leach, P. 2001. *Roman Somerset* (Dovecote Press) covers the historic county, and there are detailed publications of excavations at Bath - see Cunliffe, B. 2000. *Roman Bath Discovered* (Tempus) for an introductory account; at Ilchester: Leach, P. (1982). *Ilchester Volume I. Excavations 1974-5* (Bristol), & 1994. *Ilchester Volume 2. Excavations and Fieldwork to 1984* (Sheffield); Camerton: Wedlake, W. 1958. *Excavations at Camerton, Somerset* (Camerton); Rahtz, P. et al 2000. *Cannington Cemetery* (English Heritage); Alcock, L. 1995. *Cadbury Castle, Somerset: The Early Medieval Archaeology* (Cardiff); or Leach, P. 2001. *Fosse Lane: Excavations of a Romano-British Roadside settlement at Shepton Mallet* (The Roman Society, London), among others.

Once again, the Somerset Archaeological and Natural History Society Proceedings and those of the University of Bristol Spelaeological Society are sources for many more publications relating to the archaeology of these periods in Somerset.

Other sources and information

The Somerset County Council Historic Environment Record in Taunton holds a computerised register of all known archaeological and historic sites in the administrative county, and this can be accessed by E-mail: heritage@somerset.gov.uk or Website: www.somerset.gov.uk/heritage.

The Somerset County Museum Service in Taunton is the primary repository for archaeological finds and archives from Somerset. The Somerset and Dorset Portable Antiquities Scheme, which encourages reporting, identification and recording of archaeological finds, also operates through the museum.
E-mail: county-museums@somerset.gov.uk
Website: www.somerset.gov.uk/museums

The Somerset Archive and Record Service in Taunton preserves and makes available documents and records relating to the historic county of Somerset, and can be accessed by E-mail: archives@somerset.gov.uk
Website: www.somerset.gov.uk/archives

The Somerset Archaeological and Natural History Society based in Taunton promotes interest in local archaeology and natural history, is affiliated with many local societies around the county, publishes an annual volume of Proceedings, and has a large library.
E-mail: office@sanhs.org
Website: www.sanhs.org

The Somerset Studies Library in Taunton has comprehensive collections of books, maps, photographs and all publications relating to Somerset, which may be consulted by the public or borrowed in some instances.
E-mail: somstud@somerset.gov.uk
Website: www.somerset.gov.uk/libraries

Collections of archaeological material from Somerset are held and displayed by several museums around the region, as well as that in the County Museum at Taunton. These include the Roman Baths Museum at Bath, Bristol City Museum, Weston super Mare Museum, The Tribunal, Glastonbury, and the Wells and Mendip Museum. There are further collections and displays of material in museums at Bridgwater, Frome, Ilchester and Yeovil, and a small display of finds and information relating to the Fosse Lane settlement can be seen in the Tourist Information Centre, Shepton Mallet. See also the websites of The Beacon Hill Society for further information: www.beaconhillsocietymendip.org.uk, The Shepton Mallet Local History Society, and www.somersethistory.co.uk

Thanks

Many have contributed directly or indirectly to this publication and I am particularly grateful to somersethistory.co.uk and to Alan Stone for facilitating it, as well as for all his encouragement and assistance throughout.

Thanks also to Fred Davies, who inspired me initially to write on these topics following the discoveries at Fosse Lane in 1990, and also to other friends and colleagues in and around Shepton Mallet whom I have come to know and sometimes work with through a series of archaeology projects in the area since then.

I am grateful to the Beacon Hill Society and its members, in particular its secretary Peter Banks, for all their support and enthusiasm, as well as The Woodland Trust, in enabling the Beacon Hill Wood project.

Thanks to Somerset County Council and their officers in the Historic Environment Service and County Museum - notably Bob Croft, Steven Membery and Chris Webster, and Steven Minnitt - for support and encouragement over many years of working in Somerset.

Thanks also to Peter Ellis for his generous contribution as proof reader and for his preface, but above all as a friend and colleague for longer than either of us care to remember!

Above all I am grateful to members of my family, several of whom have participated in some of the archaeological projects featured in this book, and especially to my wife Dee who has been there for me throughout.

Picture Credits

Birmingham Archaeology: Pages 10, 20, 33, 45, 46, 56, 66, 80

Peter Leach: Cover, pages 8, 11, 12, 13, 16, 17, 19, 22, 23, 30, 32, 34, 35, 36, 37, 38, 39, 40, 41, 42, 44, 48, 49, 50, 51, 52, 55, 59, 60, 61, 62, 63, 64, 65, 66, 67, 68, 69, 71, 72, 73, 74, 76, 77, 78, 79, 81, 82, 83, 84, 85, 86, 87

Roman Baths Museum: Page 47

Somerset Archaeological and Natural History Society: pages 25, 27, 28, 50, 76

Somerset County Council: Pages 14, 15, 21, 22, 24, 53, 58, 70

Somerset County Museums: Pages 7, 31, 43, 47, 57, 70, 75

Index